Rutiodon

Written by David White
Illustrated by Pam Mara

Library of Congress Cataloging-in-Publication Data

White, David, 1952 July 13–
  Rutiodon.

  Summary: Follows Rutiodon through her day as she feeds in the river
and defends her eggs from the elements and other dinosaurs.
  1. Rutiodon—Juvenile literature.
[1. Rutiodon. 2. Dinosaurs] I. Mara, Pam, ill. II. Title.
QE862.T47W48 1988   567.9′7   87-36924
ISBN 0-86592-522-4

Rourke Enterprises, Inc.
Vero Beach, FL 32964

Quetzalcoatlus

Parasaurolphus

Deinosuchus

Corythasaurus

Spinosaurus

Oviraptor

Rutiodon

Pachycephalosaurus

Anatosaurus

Struthiomimus

Scolosaurus

Rutiodon

Psittacosaurus

As the sun rose above the horizon of the valley, the creatures of the river bank began to stir. Rutiodon was already awake. She was keeping a constant watch over the nest of eggs she had laid two days earlier. Soon, they would be ready to hatch.

Rutiodon stretched her legs, which were stiff from the cold. She was hungry after the long night. It was now time for her to go to the river to hunt for fish.

She raised herself on her four powerful legs and moved off in the direction of the river. A small Coelurosaur darted out of her path as she made her way through the ferns and horsetails. The Coelurosaur was no match for Rutiodon, who was a powerful creature. She was almost twelve feet long, with many sharp teeth in her long jaws. She was also well armored against attack.

Soon, Rutiodon reached the river. She slid into the clear waters with hardly a sound. She began to swim upstream. Only her eyes and the nostrils just in front of them appeared above the water.

Rutiodon swam swiftly, her great tail sweeping from side to side, propelling her through the water. Her long jaws snapped shut on the fish. There were plenty for her to eat. Other animals, too, were hunting the fish. On the far side of the river, Rutiodon could see a group of Cyclotosaurus in the water. There were enough fish for everyone.

When she had eaten her fill, Rutiodon returned downstream. She clambered up the bank, anxious to return to the place where her eggs were hidden. She did not dare to leave them unguarded for too long. The eggs of a Rutiodon were tempting food for many animals in the river valley.

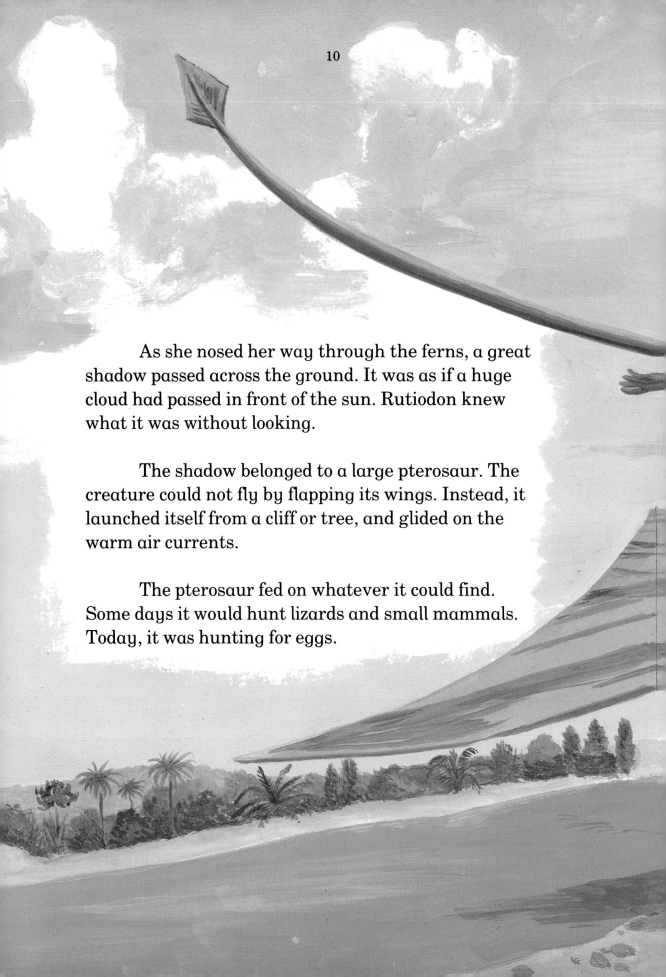

As she nosed her way through the ferns, a great shadow passed across the ground. It was as if a huge cloud had passed in front of the sun. Rutiodon knew what it was without looking.

The shadow belonged to a large pterosaur. The creature could not fly by flapping its wings. Instead, it launched itself from a cliff or tree, and glided on the warm air currents.

The pterosaur fed on whatever it could find. Some days it would hunt lizards and small mammals. Today, it was hunting for eggs.

Rutiodon moved quickly to protect her eggs. She
covered them with her great body. Hissing through her
nostrils, her jaw gaping, she warned off the pterosaur.
The creature swooped once, saw it was useless, and
backed away. Then the pterosaur disappeared to look
for easier prey .

The danger had past. Rutiodon could now doze in the midday sun while she digested her meal. Occasionally there were interruptions, and Rutiodon would half open her eyes. She saw Stagonolepis lumbering through the undergrowth. He looked threatening, with big bony plates on his back for protection. Rutiodon knew she need not fear him.

Stagonolepis was not looking for trouble. He was not interested in the eggs Rutiodon was guarding. Instead, he grubbed in the ground for the juicy roots of plants. Eventually he moved away, snuffling as he went.

The sun was now at its height. The air grew sultry. Away to the northwest, the sky began to darken. The sound of thunder rolled across the valley. Forks of lightning shot down from the upper air. Rutiodon knew instinctively what was to follow. A sudden roaring sound grew louder and louder. A flash flood was coming.

The river, swollen with rain, tumbled down the valley. Muddy water broke over the river banks and swept off anything in its way.

Rutiodon carefully put her eggs in her mouth and carried them to the safety of higher ground. Other animals were not so quick to escape. Henodus, a flat-headed creature encased in a thick shell, was swept off his rock. Mastodonsaurus, who was grazing on the river bank, struggled to stay upright as the torrent swirled around his feet. He, too, was swept downstream.

Suddenly, it was quiet. The flood subsided as quickly as it had risen. The river returned to normal. The only evidence of the flood was a thick carpet of mud spread across both banks.

Rutiodon remained near her eggs. In her new hiding place, away from the river, there were new dangers. Rutiodon could see the edge of the pine woods, where herds of Plateosaurus grazed. Suddenly, there was a sound of breaking foliage. The Plateosauruses paused in their eating, their long necks bending as they turned to see the cause of the noise.

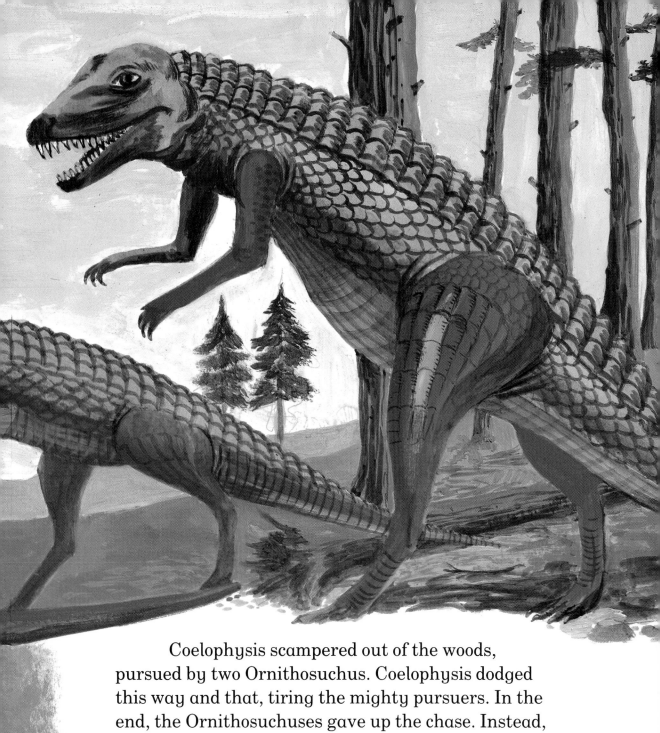

Coelophysis scampered out of the woods, pursued by two Ornithosuchus. Coelophysis dodged this way and that, tiring the mighty pursuers. In the end, the Ornithosuchuses gave up the chase. Instead, they turned on a third Ornithosuchus.

Soon the pine woods echoed with the sound of animals snapping and tearing at each other's flesh. The two Ornithosuchus finally brought down the third. The struggle was over.

However, the danger was not past for Rutiodon. Coelophysis headed straight for her after he had escaped from the Ornithosuchuses. Now he circled around the eggs, snatching and biting with his grasping claws and pointed beak. Rutiodon lunged at him angrily. Coelophysis danced away and then danced back again, looking for a way around Rutiodon.

Finally, the Coelophysis gave up. He was hungry, and he was using up valuable energy. He must find easier prey. As suddenly as he had come, he dashed off into the ferns.

Rutiodon could now relax for a while. Soon it would be night again. New dangers would appear. In the dusk, Rutiodon could again leave the eggs to go down to the river for fish. The river was calm and clear, as if the torrent of the day had never happened. Rutiodon swam lazily, enjoying the cool water. Then she returned to her eggs. For the first time that day, she slept.

Rutiodon and the Triassic Era

The skeleton of Rutiodon compared in size with a man

The time of Rutiodon

The beginning of the Mesozoic Era was the Triassic Period. It was called Triassic because three rock layers ("tri" means three) dating from this period were found in Germany.

The Triassic Period was between 225 and 193 million years ago.

Rutiodon lived during the Late or Upper Triassic Period; that is, in the second half, some 190 million years ago.

The land of Rutiodon

By the Late Triassic Period, the vast supercontinent Pangaea had split up to form Laurasian the north and Gondwanaland in the South.
Laurasia included modern North America, Europe and Asia. This is where Rutiodon lived.

Rutiodon lived near pools and rivers, just as crocodiles do today.

The family tree of Rutiodon

Rutiodon belonged to the thecodonts, or "socket-toothed" reptiles. These were a very important family since they led to the crocodiles, dinosaurs and pterosaurs.

The family tree of Rutiodon

Thecodonts evolved 226 million years ago, right at the beginning of the Triassic Period. The first were the proterosuchians. These were heavy sprawling creatures. They were followed by the pseudosuchians, which were much lighter and more nimble. Then came the aetosaurs, the armored plant eaters, and finally the flesh-eating phytosaurs.

Rutiodon was a phytosaur. Fish-eating phytosaurs dominated rivers and pools until they were replaced by crocodiles. They looked very similar to crocodiles. The only difference was that their nostrils were close to their eyes, while a crocodile's are at the end of its snout.

Other flesh eaters

During the Triassic Period, two kinds of meat eaters evolved - large and small. The small meat eaters were called coelurosaurs. They made up for their size with their speed. One of the most successful was Coelophysis. This creature was about 10 feet in length, with a long thin tail to balance it when it ran. Its bones were thin and delicate to keep its bodyweight light.

The large meat eaters were the carnosaurs. Many scientists think that Ornithosuchus was the first of the carnosaurs. It was the most fearsome dinosaur of its time. Its only real enemy was another Ornithosuchus.

Among the fish eaters was Cyclotosaurus. As large as a crocodile, Cyclotosaurus had weak legs and needed to stay in water to support its body. It opened its mouth by raising its skull rather than dropping its lower jaw.

Plant eaters

Plateosaurus was a lizard-hipped dinosaur, almost 20 feet long, that lived in the lowland swamps. It was a prosauropod and the forerunner of giants like Diplodcus. It shared its environment with numerous amphibians. Among the amphibians, Mastodonsaurus was by far the largest. Its skull alone was over three feet long.

Stagnolepis looked fiercer than it was. It was an aetorsaur, one of the armor-plated plant eaters. It had a pig-like nose and weak teeth.

Henodus was a reptile which looked like a turtle. In fact placodonts like Henodus did eventually evolve into marine turtles.

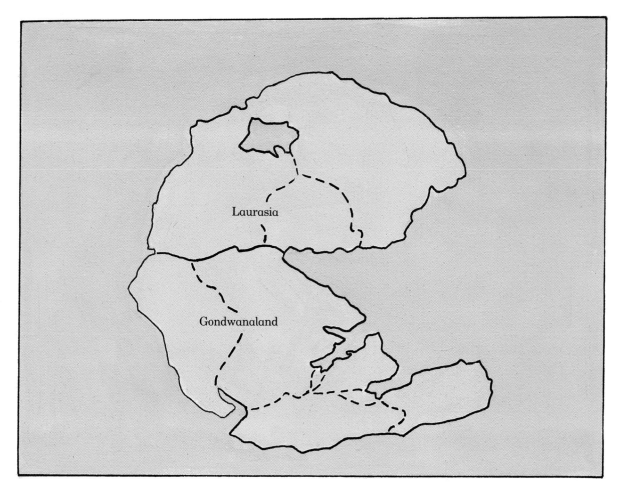

Map of the Triassic Era